LET'S  DRAW!

Sr. Sanchez
Violet Peto

ARCTURUS

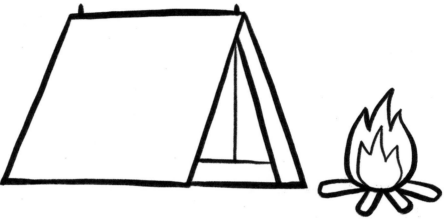

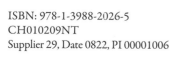

This edition published in 2022 by Arcturus Publishing Limited
26/27 Bickels Yard, 151–153 Bermondsey Street,
London SE1 3HA

Author: Lisa Regan
Illustrator: Sr. Sanchez
Editor: Violet Peto
Designer: Linda Storey
Design Manager: Jessica Holliland
Managing Editor: Joe Harris

ISBN: 978-1-3988-2026-5
CH010209NT
Supplier 29, Date 0822, PI 00001006

Printed in China

LET'S DRAW ANYTHING!

HELLO, SLEEPY HEAD!

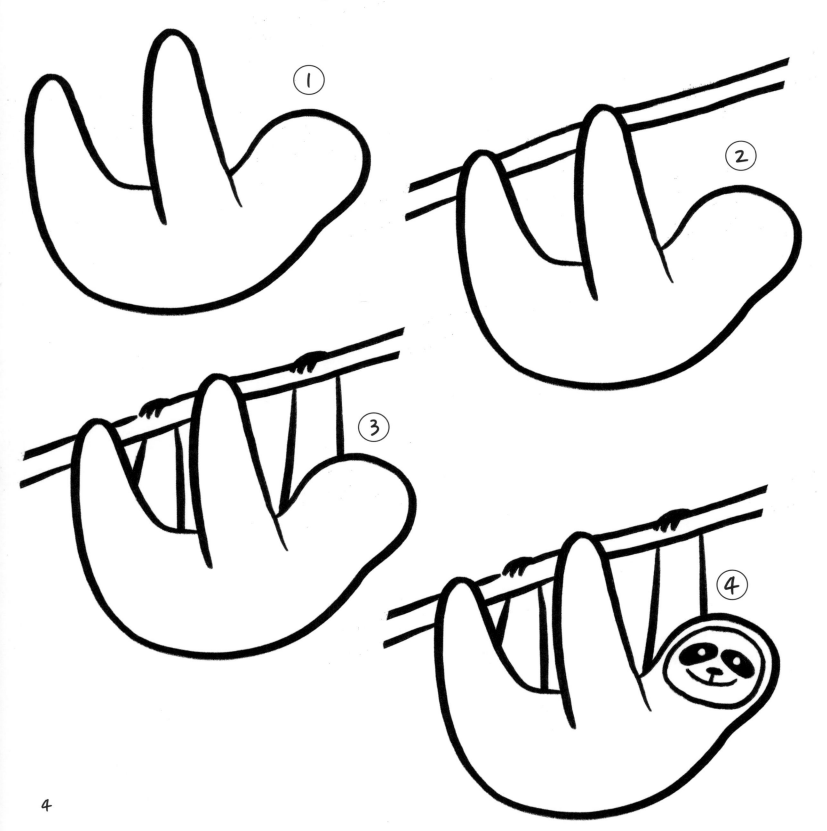

Draw a sleepy sloth friend on the other branch.

HERE COMES TROUBLE

6

Add another masked raccoon getting into mischief.

ON TOP OF THE WORLD

How many
llamas are
living here?
You decide!

NIGHTLIGHTS

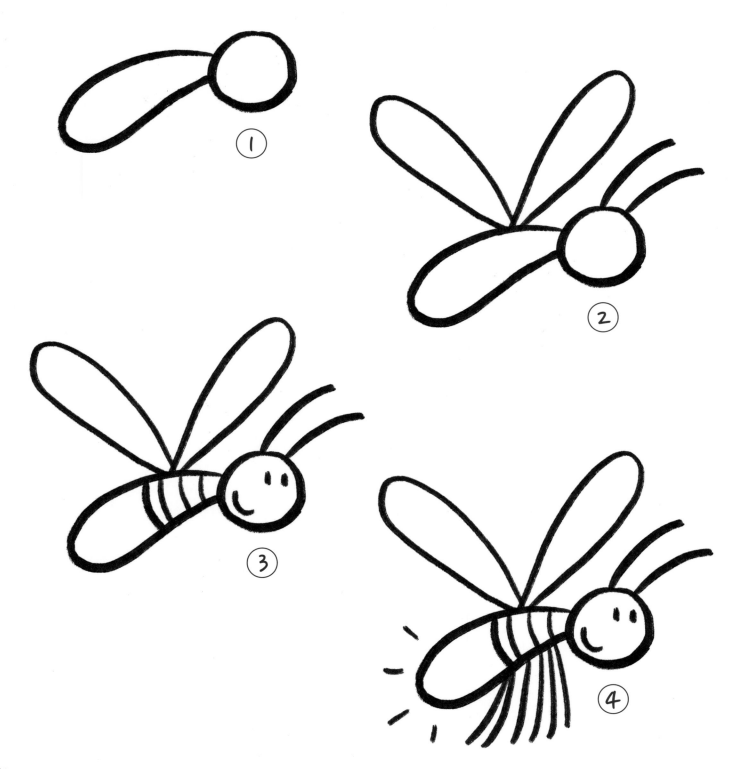

Draw lots and lots of fireflies twinkling in the dark.

A MIGHTY MANE

Give this lioness a mate.

ALL CHANGE

Use whatever shades you like for another hungry chameleon!

15

KING OF THE JUNGLE

Keep the peace by drawing some smaller gorillas in the gang.

WATCH OUT!

1
2
3
4
5
6

Draw your own crash of rhinos here.

AMAZING ANTLERS

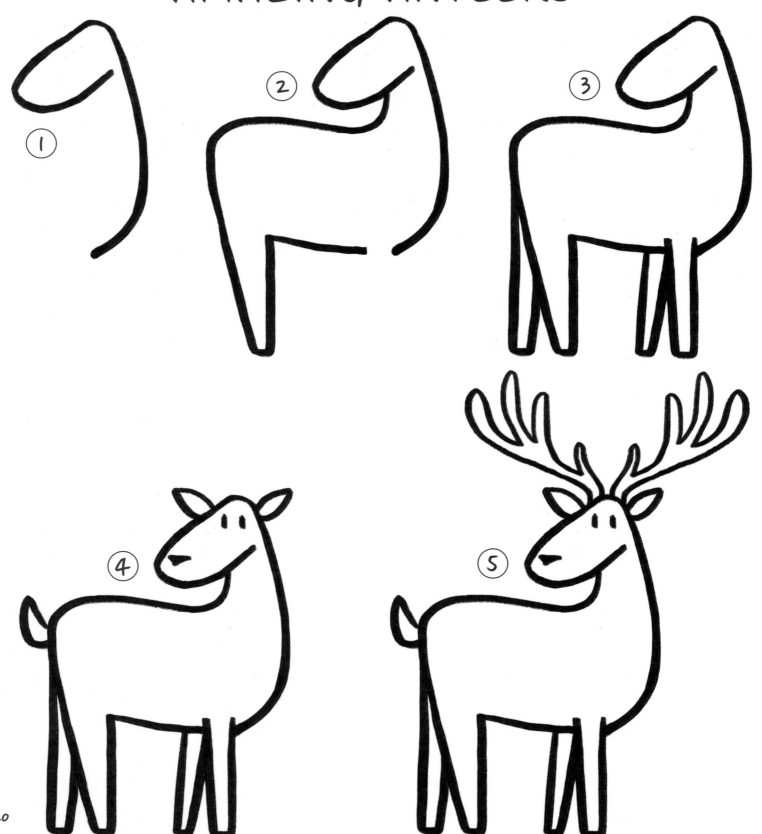

Add another stag in the clearing.
Why not draw a female deer without
antlers too?

21

LOOK BEFORE YOU LEAP

There's room for another lemur if you like!

STANDING GUARD

24

How many meerkats are on the lookout?

FEEL THE PINCH

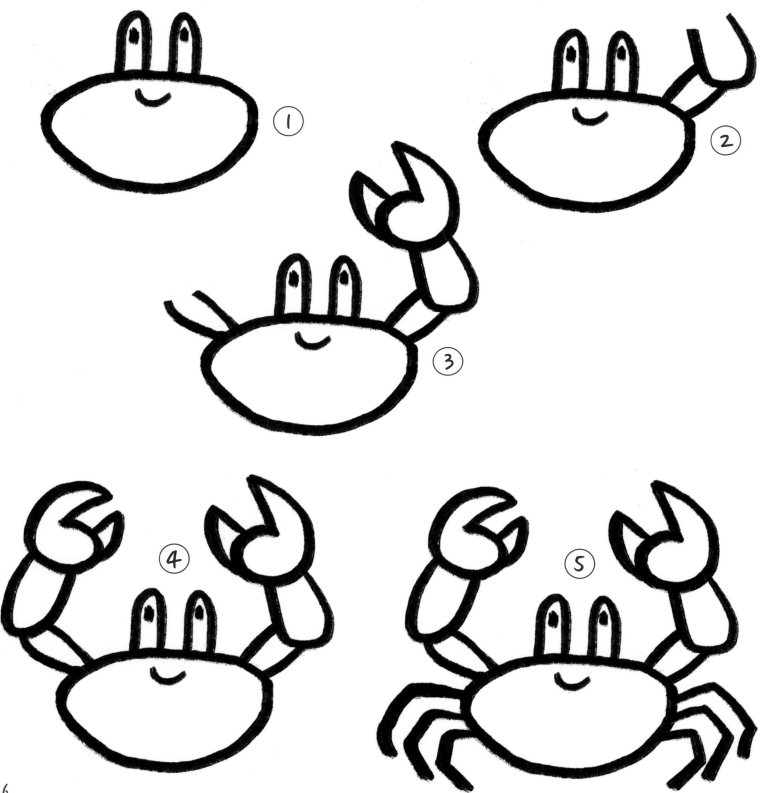

Can you fit two more crabs
scurrying in the sand?

FIT TO FIGHT

Give this kangaroo another roo to box against.

STEP BACK IN TIME

Draw a friend for this cave dweller.

FAR-FLUNG PLACES

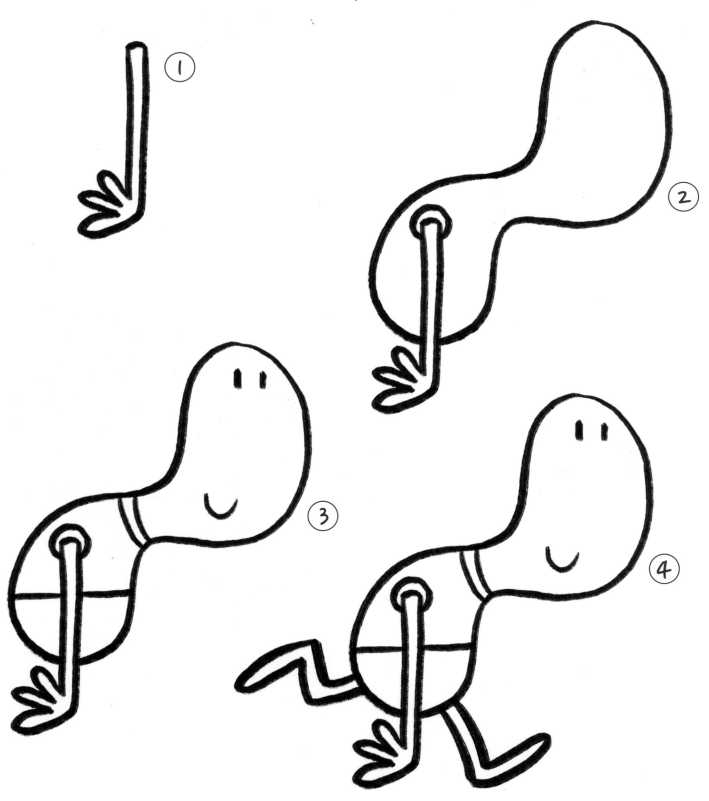

Draw another alien life form on this planet.

CUTE CRITTER

BIG BEAST

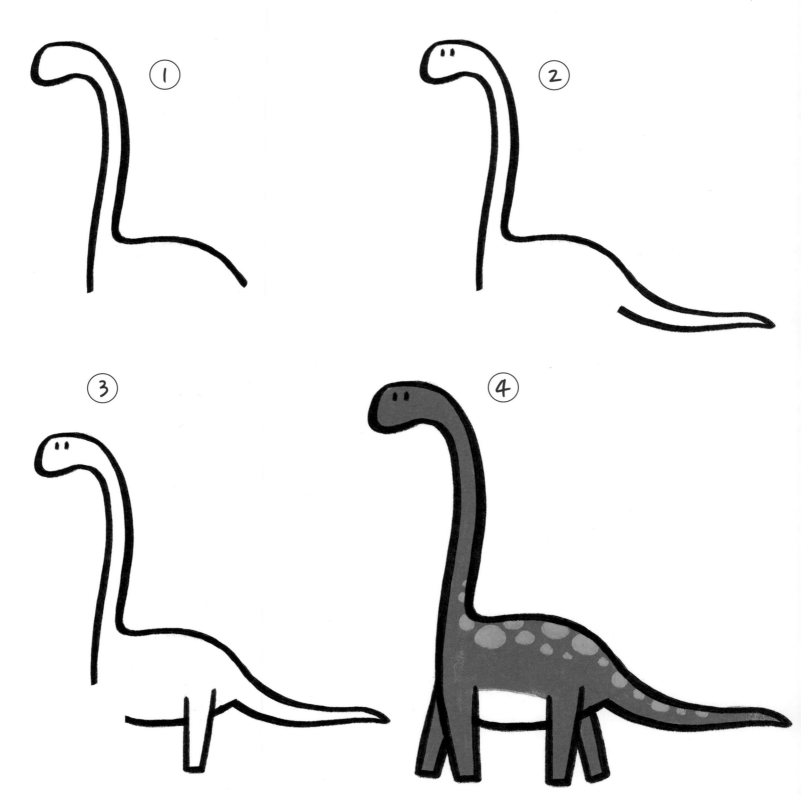

MAKE A ROBOT

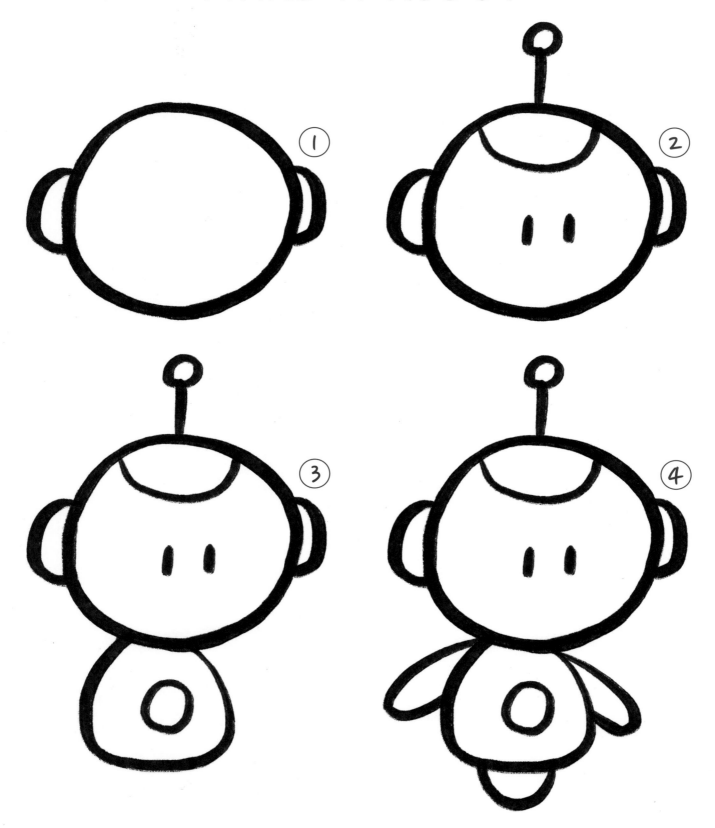

You can never have too much tech!
Draw another robot here.

WISHFUL THINKING

Add a unicorn standing proudly on the plinth!

FRIGHT NIGHT

Face your fears, and draw another vampire!

BREATHING FIRE

Draw another dragon for this one to fight.

BUILD A FORT

Can you add a fort
at the top of this hill?

FAIRY FRIENDS

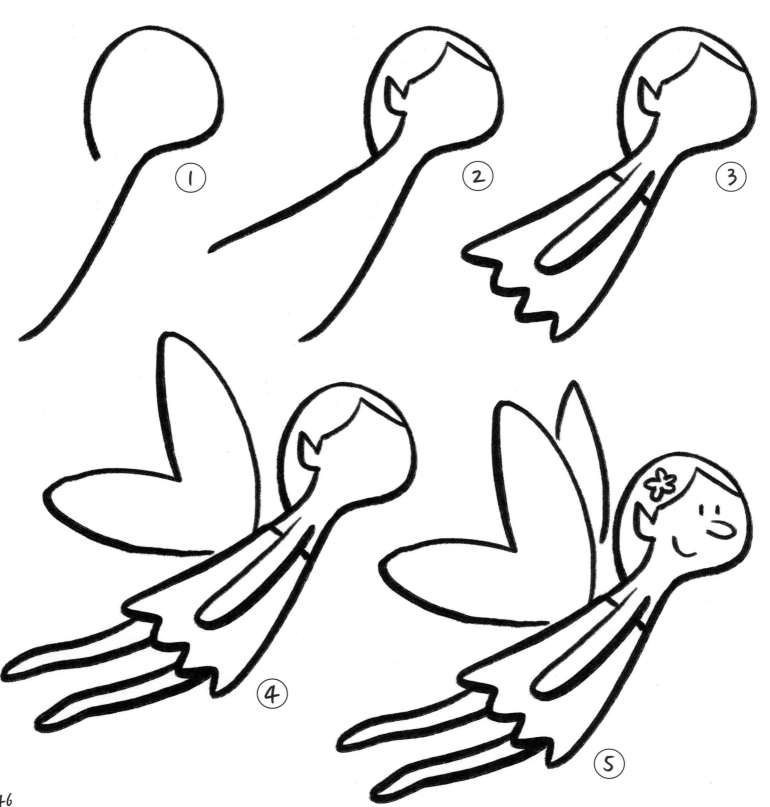

Draw another fairy fluttering by the flowers.

CAST A SPELL!

Draw lots of spell-makers
at this wizard convention.

WHATEVER THE WEATHER

Whatever the weather may be, you can draw it!

ROAR!

Watch out, there are monsters about!

Add some more here.

CIRCUS TRICKS

Add another unicyclist to this acrobatic act.

TO THE RESCUE

Quick! Send more help!

ZOOM!

①

②

③

④

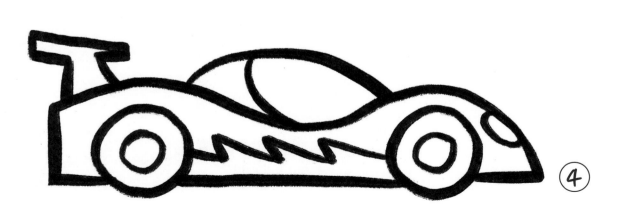

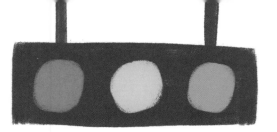

Draw another race car. Which will cross the finish line first?

INTO ORBIT

OUT OF THIS WORLD

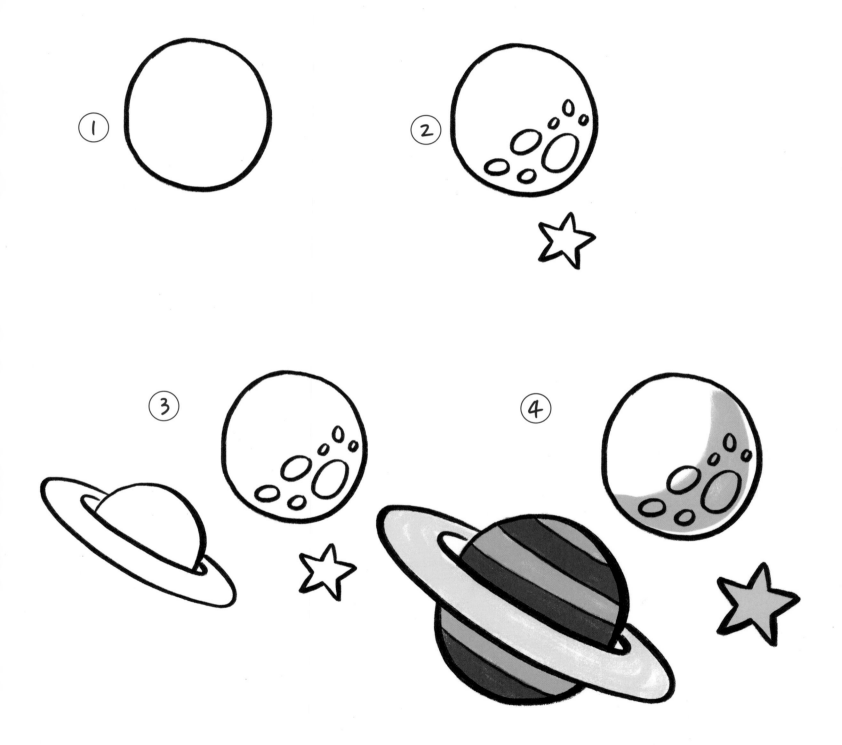

ALL AT SEA

Draw another boat to race with this one.

UP, UP, AND AWAY

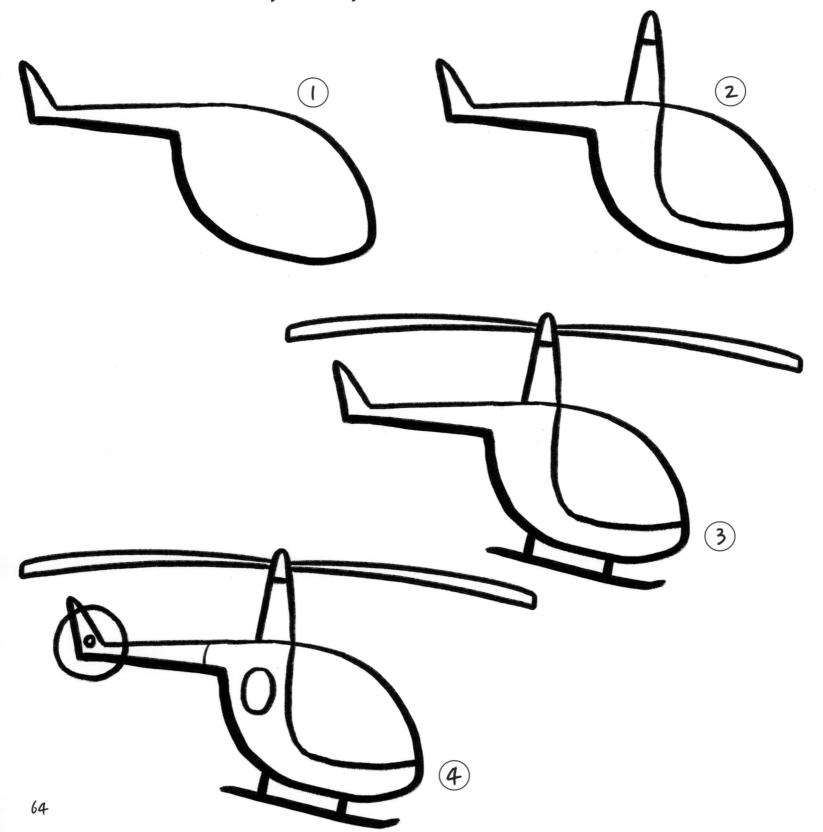

Add another helicopter
to this cityscape.

A HARD DAY'S WORK

A team of tractors gets the work done.

ON SITE

Give this dump truck a helping hand by drawing another.

AHOY THERE!

Draw a pirate ship going
into battle with this one.

ROLL WITH IT

Add some more skaters on the ramps.

73

DRIVING LESSON

Learn to draw before you drive!

PARTY TIME

TASTY TREAT

GRAB A SLICE

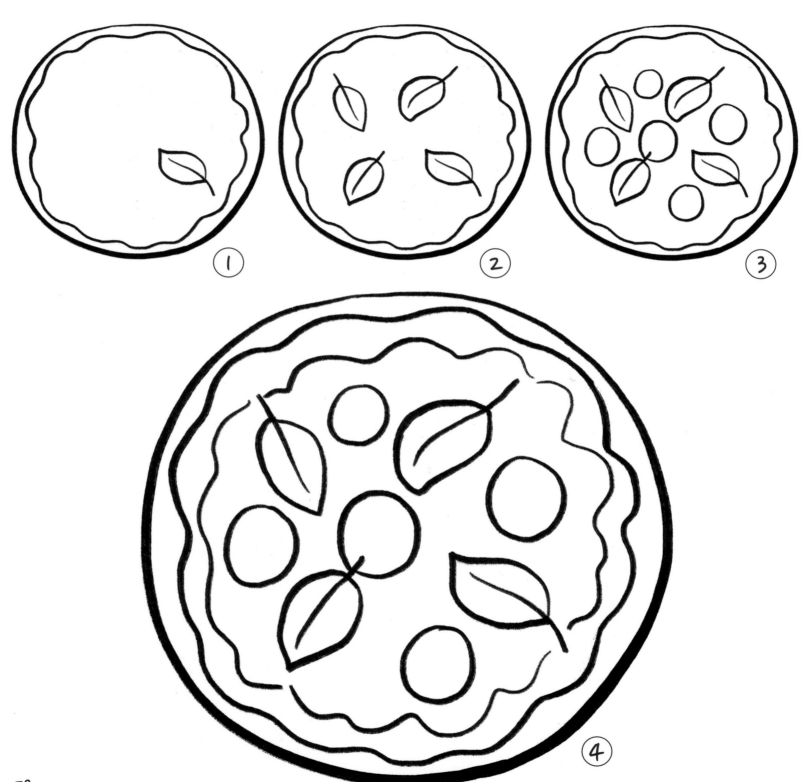

Load your pizzas with all the best toppings.

THE GREAT OUTDOORS

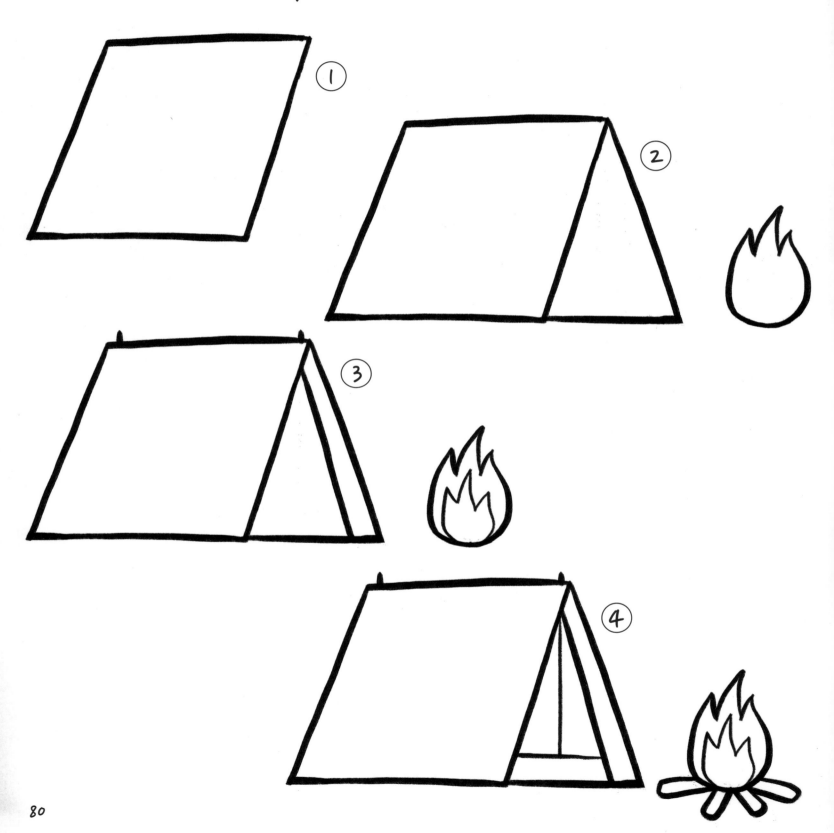

Build a bonfire for all the tents at the campsite.

PLAY BALL

1
2
3
4
5

82

Draw some teammates for Charlie!

HOMEWORK HELPER

Add a laptop to this table at the library.

PIÑA COL-ORADA

Make a pineapple pattern!

FRUITY FAMILY

1

2

3

4

5

6

Fill this page with funny fruit characters.

HEY, CHICK

Watch out, they're hatching all over the place!

CLOWNING AROUND!

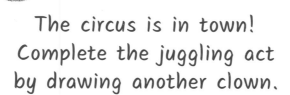

The circus is in town!
Complete the juggling act
by drawing another clown.

PURR-FECT PET

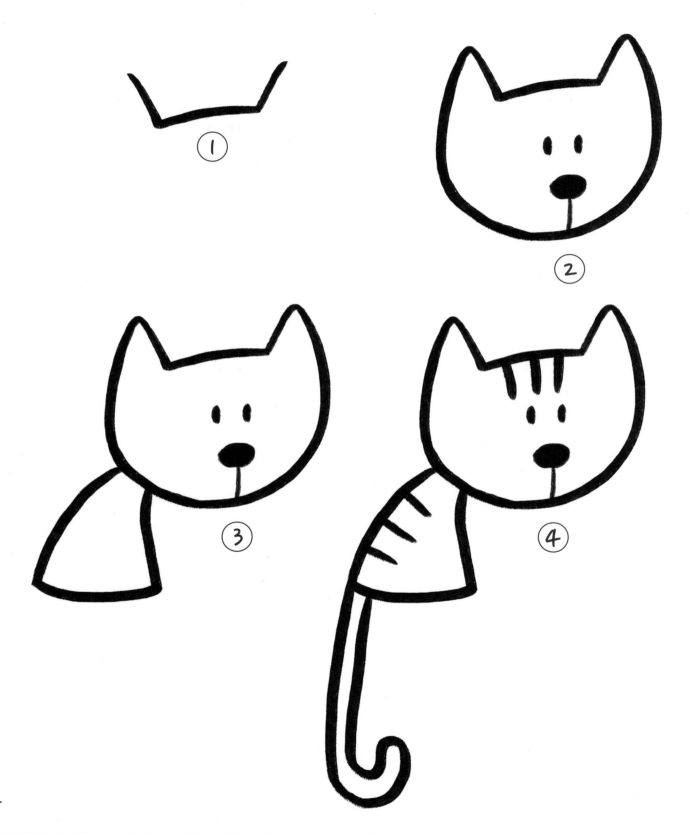

Give your pet a feline friend to relax with.

ON THE GO

Congratulations, you
have finished this book!
What will you draw next?